HAROLD BOWMAN
ON TOUR
DOWN UNDER

Compiled by

Michael E. Ulyatt

Researched by

David Bowman

Hutton Press

1992

Published by the Hutton Press Ltd.,
130 Canada Drive, Cherry Burton,
Beverley, North Humberside HU17 7SB

Typeset and printed by
Image Colourprint Ltd.
Anlaby, Hull.

ISBN 1 872167 40 3

DEDICATION

To my late Grandfather, Harold - David Bowman.

Contents

INTRODUCTION

It must have seemed an unbelievably long way from Pocklington in the East of Yorkshire, England to Cootamundra in the South East of Australia to a 21 year old farm labourer in 1924. After just two full seasons in the hard world of rugby league, Harold Bowman achieved every player's dream, selection for England to tour Australia and New Zealand.

Harold was born at 19 Rose Street, Fountain Road in the heart of Hull's industrial area on 22nd May 1902. He attended Fountain Road School until he was 13 when his parents, fearing for his delicate state of health, placed him in the country to work as a farm labourer. Presumably Harold grew in stature due to the hard work and fresh air on the farm. He also developed a love of sport, taking part in running and cycle racing events at the Burstwick and District Athletic Sports, Howden St. Peters A.F.C. Sports, the Brough and District Agricultural and Horticultural Society Evening Sports, the South Cave Fair Annual Sports and the Newport Feast Athletic Sports, whose Show President was Col. The Hon. F. S. Jackson, M.P. for Howdenshire. Educated at Harrow and Canterbury, he became a great Yorkshire County cricketer, Governor of Bengal and President of both Yorkshire C.C.C. and the M.C.C.

Cash prizes for the winners at the sports ranged from 10/- (50p) to £7/10/- (£7.50), which was worth winning in those days.

Harold also played full back for the North Newbald Village soccer club who belonged to the Beverley and District football league. However, the side were the chopping blocks of the league, losing one match 17-0 and only scoring two goals in one season! They must have been keen lads though, because they always fielded a full eleven and mostly cycled to away games, sometimes a round journey distance of sixteen miles.

Former Hull F.C. international full back, Harry Taylor, often watched the village soccer team on a Saturday afternoon. He was most impressed with the stature and enthusiastic play of Harold and suggested to his friend, Mr. J. R. Pickering, Vice-Chairman of Hull F.C., that he ought to watch the 19 year old. This he did and being impressed also, he invited Harold to the Boulevard for a series of trials where he did so well that the club's directors offered to sign him on in August 1921, becoming the youngest player then on the club's books. At 5ft. 10in. and nearly 14 stones, he made an ideal prop and adapted to rugby football league in no time at all, playing in 29 out of 37 'A' team games with three matches for the first team. His debut for the first team was against Halifax at the Boulevard on 10th December 1921 when the team was:- Rogers, Holdsworth, Kennedy, Batten, Mills, Milner and Charles, Bowman, Ellis, Grice, Taylor, Garratt and Wyburn. The referee was Rev. F. Chambers of Dewsbury.

The unassuming youngster was keen to learn and received great help from established first teamers Wyburn, Beasty, Oliver and Milner. In 1923 he became engaged to Miss Eileen Margaret Todd, daughter of Councillor Todd of Pocklington and they married on 2nd April 1924.

Harold now travelled to some matches by motorcycle, a Triumph, reg. no. AT 8060. His form was so improved he was selected for two international trial matches in early winter 1924 at Headingley and Wigan. Two good games meant that the selectors picked him for the summer tour of Australia and New Zealand, the club's first Hull-born tourist. The club's directors supplied complete clothing outfits for Harold. The team manager on the tour, J. H. (Harry) Dannatt, was mine host of the Shipping Office Hotel in Posterngate, Hull (advertising slogan: "Matches re-played every Sunday"), as well as a director of Hull F.C.

Harold Bowman had the good sense to keep diaries, photographs, tour itineraries, press cuttings, shipboard menus and programmes on the 1924 and 1928 tours of Australia and New Zealand.

Family group in 1904. Harold is sat on his mother's knee.

Harold in his early days at Hull.

North Newbald Football Club, 1918. Harold Bowman is seated far right.

*Double Wedding Day,
2nd April 1924.*

*Harold and Eileen (centre right)
with best man Stan Whitty.*

*Harold and Eileen on
their wedding day.*

*Fred Bowman (Harold's father)
and best man Stan Whitty.*

TOUR IN AUSTRALIA AND NEW ZEALAND IN 1924

Since the success of the first Lions tour in 1910 it had always been the aim of every Rugby League player to gain selection for an Australasian tour. Selection meant a lot more than the opportunity to play rugby league at the highest level, it gave many young men their only chance to travel to the other side of the world.

Harold had had an outstanding season in 1923/24. He helped Hull to a Yorkshire Cup Final win when they beat Huddersfield 10-4 at Headingley before a crowd of 23,493. He also played for Yorkshire twice that season, against Cumberland at Hunslet and against Lancashire at Oldham. Two tour trial matches were held, at Headingley on January 9th and at Wigan on February 20th. The official tour party was announced on February 27th. It was:- J. Parkin (capt.) and C. Pollard (Wakefield Trinity), W. Burgess and C. Carr (Barrow), T. Howley, D. Hurcombe, J. Price and J. Sullivan (Wigan), E. Knapman, S. Rix, R. Sloman and A. Brough (Oldham), J. Thompson and J. Bacon (Leeds), W. Bentham (Broughton Rangers), W. Cunliffe (Warrington), D. Rees (Halifax), B. Gronow (Huddersfield), W. Mooney and J. Darwell (Leigh), J. Bennett (Rochdale Hornets), F. Evans (Swinton), F. Gallagher (Batley), H. Bowman and S. Whitty (Hull). Managers:- J. H. Dannatt (Hull) and E. Osborne (Warrington). Trainer:- D. Murray.

John Wilson, Secretary of the Rugby Football League, wrote to all players on behalf of the Council of the Rugby League from 84 Grange Avenue, Leeds on 6th March 1924 inviting all twenty six players to tour Australasia but asking them to keep the terms private.

Each player received an allowance of £1 per week on board ship and £2 per week on shore, £10 in a lump sum before New Zealand and one third of the profits of the tour shared equally among all 26 players on the tour, £2 per week to player's wives and 7/6d (37$\frac{1}{2}$p) per week for each child under 14.

Players had to provide boots and a pair of knee bandanges. The R.L. Council provided blazers and straw boaters but each player was asked to be well and smartly dressed and take two suits, a spare pair of trousers to wear with the blazer, two pairs of pyjamas, at least six shirts with spare collars (soft or stiff preferred), two pairs of boots or shoes, white deck shoes, six pairs of socks, underwear, house shoes, overcoats (heavy and light), shaving tackle, hair, boot and clothes brushes, cap, two suits of white drill for going through the hot zone, cabin trunk (not more than 15" high) and a suitcase.

Yorkshire based players were requested to meet at the Griffin Hotel in Leeds on Friday March 14th to fill in passport forms and to bring with them six unmounted photographs and three postcard photographs of themselves "to distribute to the press in Australia and New Zealand". The Lancashire and Cumberland players met at the Victoria Hotel in Manchester on Wednesday 19th March.

The world travel arrangements were made by Thomas Cook and Son Ltd. of Piccadilly, London W1, and all mail en route could be forwarded to Wellington, San Francisco, Chicago, New York or Liverpool.

Harold had his photographs for the tour taken by Norman L. Brook, Photographer of Pocklington, at a cost of £1/13/6d (£1.67). Hull F.C. directors and club supporters rallied round magnificently, "I received complete outfits from the directors and useful gifts from the shareholders and supporters of the club". His club colleague Stan Whitty received the same.

George Miller, Chairman of Hull F.C. and a partner in the Hull Solicitors, Middlemiss, Pearce and Miller, wrote to Harold congratulating him "on an honour well deserved and is a result of your good conduct on and off the field". Strangely, Miller headed his letter "Dear Bowman".

The Norwood R.F.C., whose headquarters were at the Rose and Crown Hotel in West Street, Hull, also wrote to Harold, congratulating him on his selection and wishing him a pleasant and enjoyable tour.

Harold and Stan Whitty left Hull's Paragon Station at 10.00 am on April 10th and met up with the Yorkshire players at Doncaster before travelling onto Kings Cross where they stayed at the St. Pancras Hotel. The other players had already arrived and after settling in, Harold and Stan were entertained to the Coliseum Theatre by ex-Barrow director Mr. Thomas Taylor, together with their "cabin mates to-be" Burgess and Carr. On the Friday the whole party travelled to Tilbury Docks to board the S.S. "Moldavia". The players were in great demand from press photographers, such was the interest in the tour. After lunch at 1 p.m., the "Moldavia" sailed at 2 p.m. The pilot came on board at Dover and took letters off. Harold began unpacking some of his things and pushed his cabin trunk beneath his bunk before reading his Ocean Accident and Guarantee Corporations player and baggage insurance policy!

The party went to bed at around 10.30 p.m. "We all feared the Bay of Biscay crossing", wrote Harold. "At breakfast time the wind had

A cartoon by Ern Shaw in Hull F.C.'s Centenary Year.

Right:

Stan Whitty, Mr. Dannatt and Harold on the deck of the 'Moldavia'.

Below:

Some of the players and officials on board the 'Moldavia' shortly before leaving Tilbury Docks.

freshened and I felt terrible and stayed in bed". The sea was very rough and few of the party ventured forth from their cabins. Mr. Dannatt found his sea legs immediately. "At breakfast and lunchtime there were very few of our party to be seen and at dinner, only nine of us out of 23 sat down. Thompson was very bad and wanted someone to take him home to die! Gronow, Burgess and Gallagher were also poorly. On Sunday the wind had dropped. We passed Cape Finestere Light and we had a very fine run down the Portugal coast, passing very close to Cape St. Vincent and seeing the entrance to Lisbon. Soon we are due at Gibraltar and then to Marseille to pick up the victors and victims of last Saturday's cup tie".

En route to Marseille, Osborne and Dannatt obtained permission for the players to get in a bit of training running around the deck of the first class department but only on condition they finished by 8 a.m. The "Moldavia" had no gymnasium but Jonty Parkin organised a sports committee to run deck games after they left Marseille. The five Wigan players and the four from Oldham who had played in the Challenge Cup Final, won by Wigan, arrived at Marseille by train. Harold wrote to the Hull Evening News, "It is becoming difficult to carry through with the rigours of training, owing to the hardness of the decks and the intensity of the heat. We now have sharp walks and play tennis, which is very good training. We also have a bit of ball practice with a large rope ball weighing about three stone".

The team had a tour of Marseille by charabanc. They visited the Notre Dame de la Gorde by way of La Prado on the top of a hill overlooking the bay, venturing up by way of a powerful hydraulic lift. As they got out of the cage lift at the top, Billy Cunliffe was first out with the comment "Hand in your miner's lamps, boys". The next day in port, the players visited the Chateau d'If, made famous by the suffering and remarkable escape of the "Count of Monte Cristo". Mr. Osborne gave the tram conductor 2 francs to pay for the whole party. "How many washers will I get in change?" he asked. This set all the players laughing as the lower values in French currency had a hole in the centre to allow them to be threaded together. The conductor got his own back by gravely handing Mr. Osborne an assortment of Greek, Latin and Spanish coins. A few of the lads bought yellow spectacles to protect their eyes from the sun, but most of their colleagues thought they looked like Harold Lloyd!

Life on board seemed varied. Gallagher opened his cabin's port hole while in harbour and Frankie Evans dreamt that night that water came in! They ran a tote each day on the knots the ship sailed every day. 298 the first day, 342 and then 369. Mr. Dannatt seemed to win on most days. Some porpoises basked alongside and even a shark was spotted. Jonty Parkin played the piano most nights and Mr. Dannatt sang. Life belt drill was instructed by the captain and deck quoits and bullboard competitions began. Parkin excelled at both.

Harold kept daily notes together with copies of reports sent back to the Hull newspaper by Stan Whitty and those wired through from Jonty Parkin to the Yorkshire Evening Post:- "APRIL 19th, Mr. Dannatt (Chairman), Mr. Watson (Secretary), Parkin and Gronow (Committee) plus two lady passengers and two gentlemen passengers were appointed to act as committee to organise games, dancing, concerts and whist drives. Gallagher won the first whist drive. Mr. Harvey of Wigan gave a champagne party to celebrate his teams' Cup Final win.

Went past that volcano Stomboli. Someone said it was erupting. We all dashed on deck but it turned out to be the moon rising! APRIL 23rd. Port Said. Visited the British hospital. Doctor in charge once played half back for Oxford. Goats run round streets like our dogs do. Back on board, an Arab climbed up the side of the ship and said he would dive off the top deck into the harbour for a few pennies. After making a good collection, he slid down a rope into a waiting boat and made his getaway. Dozens of men and boys swam out to the ship and dived for coins we threw overboard. After dinner, a party of theatricals on their way to Australia gave turns. Walter Mooney dressed up and sang comic songs. Mr. Dannatt, Darwell, Cunliffe and Brough gave songs. Good concert. W. Burgess and lady won the mixed doubles tennis, W. Burgess the singles tennis, C. Carr and Mr. Dannatt the mens double deck quoits, J. Parkin and lady the mixed doubles deck quoits, B. Gronow the singles deck quoits and J. Parkin the Deck Bullboard. APRIL 26th. Passed the chain of small rocky islands known as the Twelve Apostles. Picked up the lights of Aden. Port's surgeon came on board. One of the passengers, a Mrs. Priddle, had died on board and Mr. Osborne and Mr. Fillan represented the team at her funeral at the Civic Cemetery. (Mr. Fillan was the Huddersfield member of the R.L. Council). She had died of double pneumonia. Rest of the party went ashore for about three hours. Showed passports for the first time since we left Tilbury. Natives offered us ostrich feathers, amber necklaces, eggs, strings of beads (made in Birmingham!), cheap cigars and cigarettes. Went into a pub where a kind of show was on. For a shilling, we were told we could see real mermaids but when we got into the room all we saw were boxes containing some stuffed things which we were told were mermaids, but they were Dugongs, stuffed as well, a sort of sea cow. Left at 4.30 p.m. Four players were reported missing when we had sailed but to the great relief of the managers, they were eventually found asleep on the top deck. One or two of our party not feeling well lately and the ship's doctor said it was due to lack of training, so training started. Running, skipping, medicine ball and swedish drill at 6.30 a.m.

Cricket match between first and second class passengers. Second class scored 94 (Bacon 38, Sloman 15, Cunliffe 12, Oligey 13,

Palmer 9, Carr 4, Gronow 3, Whitty, Rise, Bentham and Thompson ducks). First class only scored 51. Ships entertainers 'The Moldovians' put on a concert. MAY 4th. Landed at Colombo at 4.30 a.m. in heavy rain and thunder after passing submarines the K.26 and L.20. Asked if we could look around the subs but the officer in charge was unable to grant our request. Ashore we made our way to the Grand Oriental Hotel where we bought English newspapers. Found out that Batley had beaten Wigan in the League Final. Gallagher said that's what he expected! Some of the party went to Kandy in Ceylon, while most of us took sightseeing tours by rickshaw or motor to the Cinnamon Gardens, the Governor's residence of Queen's House and the Black Tower Lighthouse. Gardens reminded some of us of the Valley Gardens in Harrogate. Pollard and Thompson bought two large elephants and had to have another cabin on board ship to keep them in."

Harold wrote home to his parents:-

"We went to a Buddhist's Temple in Colombo and before entering we had to take our shoes off. I got part of a zoo! I bought twelve elephants (not live ones) made of ebony and ivory. Thousands of coconut trees and pineapples are 3d each. I shall be pleased to get to Sydney to get some news from the old country. Oh, I nearly forgot to tell you, I have not been sea sick the whole of the journey."

Diary notes continued "Most police are Malay and wear a small cap gaily embroidered. The people who are most interesting are the Kabuloes, big men from the North West Frontier of India who wear velvet waistcoats, white baggy pyjama trousers and a turban wrapped around a peaked cap. Colombo is one of the prettiest places we all have ever seen.

At 10 p.m. we sailed into the Indian Ocean. Very choppy. Lightening lit up the sky for miles around.

Crossed "the line" but the usual Neptune ceremony didn't take place. Mr. Dannatt and Mr. Fillan seemed pleased they wouldn't be getting a cold water ducking! Weather getting cooler which suits us all. Burgess and Brough still feeling under the weather. Received a Marconigram from the Australian Olympic team en route to Paris, read "Best wishes for a successful trip". Nice of them. We are nearing Fremantle after nine days at sea, the longest period we have spent at sea since leaving London.

The second series of games were completed and many of the prizes were taken by our boys:-

Whist Drive - C. Pollard, Deck Tennis - J. Parkin and S. Rix, Deck Quoits - J. Bennett and J. Harvey, Bull Board - J. Ring, Bull Board (men's doubles) - J. Thompson and H. Bowman. MAY 13th. Arrived at South Wharf, Fremantle. Because of customs, cigarettes up from 2/9d (14p) to 4/6d (22$\frac{1}{2}$p) for 50. Whisky 7/6d (37$\frac{1}{2}$p) a bottle. We had to be checked out by port doctor and quarantine

officials before going onshore. We were overwhelmed by reporters and photographers. Mr. and Mrs. Pearce from Huddersfield took some of the players on a motor tour of Perth, about 12 miles away. Saw "The Soldiers Avenue" in King's Park. English oaks about 8 to 10 feet high planted every ten yards to represent a fallen soldier in the Great War who came from Western Australia. Beautiful view from here of Fremantle across the Swan River. Saw the wonder Post Office in Perth, said to have cost an incredible £5$\frac{1}{2}$M. Other players went to cinema in Fremantle. Sailed late at night, entered the Bight in very rough weather. Sixteen missing from lunch table today. Charlie Pollard's cure for sea sickness, eat plenty of fish, didn't work!

Docked at Port Adelaide at 8.30 a.m. on the Sunday. Jim Bacon so upset he had no mail waiting that he sat down and wrote himself a letter! Had a full practice match on a local soccer ground for an hour then hot bath and into Adelaide by train. Beautiful place, built in the shape of a cross. Very wide streets and lovely parks. Visited Glenelg on Holdfast Bay, birthplace of the state."

Mr. Dannatt introduced Harold and Stan to a Mr. Anson and his wife who used to live in Argyle Street, Hull." Sailed from Adelaide at 8.30 p.m., one and a half days sailing to Melbourne where we were besieged by photographers.

Crowds are booming in Sydney evidently. Settled into the Hotel Windsor then went by motors to Melbourne Cricket ground for full practice and photo call for the 17 players staying in Melbourne. First time an England side will have played here. Smothered our faces in iodine to protect against sun.

I met a young fellow named Lambert who is a farm student here but his father has a grocers shop near Division Road on Hull's Hessle Road.

At a dinner given by the New South Wales R.F.L., Harry Sunderland, President of the Victorian R.L., advised us not to heed barrackers who called us 'Pommies'. "Remember Captain Cook, if he hadn't planted the Union Jack here, Australia might have become a Dutch dependency".

Visited the "Herald" offices on the corner of Collins Place and Flinders Street where cartoonist Sam Wells sketched Jonty Parkin with hair so long Jonty went straight out and had it cut!

MAY 24th. The first match of the tour was held on the Fitzroy Cricket ground against Victoria. Our team was:- Sullivan, Rix, Bacon, Howley, Ring, Gronow, Cunliffe, Bowman, Sloman, Thompson, Gallagher, Hurcombe and Parkin (Capt.). Before the match, a goal kicking contest was held with Sullivan, Gronow, Stott (Victoria) and Robertson (South Melbourne). Sullivan kicked all his three attempts and won a gold medal and the ball which is to have a silver plate attached with his name engraved on it and the

Right:
In tropical gear on deck.

S.15278.   P & O. S. S. "MOLDAVIA" 16,000 TONS GROSS REGISTER.

P&O S.S. 'Moldavia'.

The Hull trio 'somewhere in the tropics'.

The Great Britain Team.

From right to left:
Dog Mascot, Jonty Parkin,
J. Darwall, Jim Sullivan,
Harold Bowman,
J. Thompson, G. C. Pollard,
W. H. Pullein, W. Cunliffe,
Dai Rees, J. Bennett,
Stan Whitty, T. Howley,
F. Evans.

Australian and British flags.

A crowd of around 15,000 saw the Earl of Stradbroke lay a silk Australian flag across Parkin's shoulders to mark Empire Day. The Victorians kicked off but it was obvious their forwards were too small. Slick handling brought tries to Hurcombe, Bacon, Ring (2), Bowman (2), Parkin (3), Rix and Gallagher and Sullivan kicked six goals. A worrying feature was that Victoria had nearly 30 penalties and England none. The pack played well within themselves but the three quarters were dazzling. Receipts at the match approached £800. The day after the match, members of the party were entertained at the Collingwood Football rooms. A programme including a boxing bout between Parkin and his Vice-Captain was enjoyed by all. Mr. Fillan paid tribute to the Australians, "the world's champion sportsmen". In the afternoon we motored to Sassafras. Left Melbourne for Sydney by express train about 5 p.m. Monday. Arrived at Albury at 10.30 p.m. and changed for Cootramundra, arriving there at 3 a.m., Tuesday. Entertained to a civic reception at noon. Tell us they make the finest butter in the world here. Town has around 2,500 population, but there must have been 6,000 at the game. We won 31-4. Wonderful banquet and dancing after the match. Left by train for Sydney at 3 a.m., arriving there at noon to be met by Mr. Dannatt and the other boys. Another civic reception at the Town Hall and then onto the Roseberry Park Racing Club for an enjoyable afternoon. Trained next day then entertained by New South Wales committee, one of them presented Jim Sullivan with a large 'dummy' with him being the baby of the party. MAY 31st. A crowd of over 7,000 saw us beat Newcastle 43-18. "The English forwards were again dominant but the tourists over-elaborated and were frequently penalised. They only led 13-8 at the interval and then had Bacon sent off before going behind 18-16. The tourists superior fitness told in the end. A feature of the match was the constant chorus singing of the English party watching. Bacon later received a caution from the Newcastle League. Receipts of £695. "JUNE 2nd. Charlie Carr attained his 21st birthday today, leaving Jim Sullivan the only member of the team under 21. JUNE 3rd. Left Sydney at 8 a.m. for Tamworth by train, arriving there at 8 p.m. Lord Mayor welcomed the party at the Town Hall next morning. Match kicked off at 2 p.m. at The Oval. We played a fast open game before a record crowd. Mooney, Whitty, Ring, Bacon and Pollard played well in our 34-17 victory over New England. Whitty scored 2 tries and Craig gave him his jersey after the match.

After an official reception on the night, we left for Sydney next morning. Parking remarked how Australians enjoyed "booming" their town, everyone wanted to sing the praises of their particular area. Moved to new diggings near to the beach at Brighton-le-Sands. A crowd of 41,657 saw the next match against New South Wales when thirty nine penalties were dished out against us. Despite this, we won 10-5. Gate receipts were £4,100.

The long awaited meeting of Hull's former Aussie players took place on the Saturday after the game. Fred Samuels is employed in the steel works here. Sid Dean, Andy Morton, Dinny Campbell and Jimmy Deveraux, together with their wives, met up with Mr. Dannatt, me and Stan. Due to illness, Bert Gilbert had to call off. Bert had played for Souths, Wests and St. George and was later coach to St. George. He toured England with Australia in 1911/12 before joining Hull, and he was the first colonial player to receive the R.L. Challenge Cup when Hull beat Wakefield Trinity 6-0 in the Final at Halifax in 1914. All the Australians asked to be remembered to the friends they had made in Hull during their time in England. After a five hour dinner and chat, we made our way back to the team's hotel. On the Sunday Mr. Harvey of Wigan took us for a motor car tour. We covered a distance of 150 miles, seeing some beautiful scenery. In the evening we enjoyed a sing-song around our pianola at the hotel. Charlie Pollard brought the post in, all for Whitty including Hull Sports Mails!

On Monday we were again at the Sydney Cricket Ground. Incidentally it was the King's Birthday. We played with only twelve men when Bacon was injured in the sixth minute and he took no further part in the match. New South Wales led 33-8 before we scored two late tries to finish 33-18 losers. The crowd was 37,000. JUNE 10th. Left for Queensland leaving Bacon, Bentham, Hurcombe and Price behind nursing injuries. The five hundred mile trip proved dreary. Twenty seven hour journey via Newcastle, Wallingarra and Toowoomba. JUNE 12th. We felt at home in the mud at Ipswich, their captain sportingly said he had never seen such a brilliant display as we gave in a 17-0 victory before a drenched crowd of 2,000. Talk about sunny Queensland, it was like playing at York after a few week's rain! At least we saw a Tom Mix film at the local cinema!

Next day off to Brisbane where we were welcomed by ex-Hull three-quarter Tommy Hopkins, a relation of Dave and George Ablett, Hull publicans. Originally from Wales, he now has a tin manufacturing business which we toured. Visited The Tivoli in the evening. Our hotel is the Hotel Daniel in George Street.

We lost to Queensland 10-25 before a crowd of 40,000 although we played well. Feature was how many women were at the Exhibition Grounds, paying 4s/4d. (22p) to see the match. Gallagher captained the side in Parkin's absence. Mooney had an outstanding match. Entertained after the match by the Brisbane Rugby League, then on Sunday went on a train trip to Cleveland, a seaside resort about thirty miles from Brisbane. On the Monday we went to the Empire Theatre.

Cartoonist Sam Wells' impressions of the match against Victoria.

Right:

The four "babies" of the team.

*(left to right) Jim Sullivan (20), C. W. Carr (21),
J. Thompson (21) and Harold (21).*

Below:

*Lord Stradbroke, Governor of Victoria, presents Jonty
Parkin with a silk Australian flag before the match against
Victoria. The flag was autographed by every team the
tourists met. Mr. Flowers, M.L.C., patron of the New South
Wales Rugby League (left) watches the presentation.*

JUNE 17th. Left Brisbane at 8 a.m. for Toowoomba. Arrived at noon for a reception at the Town Hall and then walked behind a brass brand to a newly opened outfitter's shop belonging to Duncan Thompson, the Australian half-back, who toured England in 1920. Mr. Dannatt officially opened the shop. Next day we met Toowoomba in a really hard match. Mooney was again outstanding but we lost 20-23 before a crowd of 10,000 who paid £950. Mr. Dannatt and Mr. Fillan later met officials of New South Wales and Queensland to interpret rule variations while the players had a meeting with some referees to iron out rule problems. Magnificent ball after the match in aid of the St. Vincents Hospital. THURSDAY JUNE 19th, left at 12 noon by train. Parkin caused a great deal of amusement when he put two large grasshoppers in Bowman's sleeping berth. Harold shot out of bed and wouldn't go back until they had been killed. He said they were as big as rabbits! Mooney killed them by stamping on them but Sullivan and Bowman didn't get any sleep. Arrived back at our hotel at lunchtime on the Friday. "Mr. Dannatt, Whitty and Bowman were sorry to learn of Bill Batten's transfer from Hull to Wakefield Trinity." 21st JUNE. Showing a vast improvement, we gained a decisive victory over New South Wales at Sydney 43-5 before a crowd of 26,042. However the Sky Blues were without seven of their players who had been selected for Australia in the Test Match on Monday June 23rd.

The Lord Mayor of Hull, Coun. E. E. Keighley, cabled Mr. Dannatt "Best wishes from the city for the success of the British team in the First Test Match".

Whitty ate twenty eight oranges when we visited a fruit farm. He is now known as the "Orange King". Stan and I spent a day at the home of Jimmy Deveraux, enjoying Yorkshire Puddings for dinner. Jimmy coaching South Sydney".

A crowd of 50,000 saw the following teams take the field in the First Test Match at Sydney:- England: J. Sullivan, S. Rix, T. Howley, C. Carr, J. Ring, D. Hurcombe and J. Parkin (capt.), W. Cunliffe, J. Bennett, W. Burgess, J. Darwell, J. Price and F. Gallagher. Australia: Fravenfelder, Blinkhorn, Horder, Gorman, Aynsley, Blair and Craig (capt.), Oxford, Watt, Potter, Bennett, O'Connor and Latta. The referee was T. McMahon.

Sullivan began his Test career by landing a 60 yard goal with his first kick and kicked 5 goals in all which with tries from Parkin (2), Rix and Price gave the Lions a 22-3 victory . "Mr. Dannatt met a Mrs Currie who had left Hull in 1880 and she cried when he told her how Hull had grown.

The following Wednesday it was a 200 mile trip to Orange through the Blue Mountains. "Welcome to Wales" was chalked in Welsh on a train in the sidings. A crowd of 10,000 saw us gain control in the later stages to win 42-23. Brough (3), Carr (2),

Thompson, Bowman and Pollard scored tries and Sullivan kicked nine goals. A dinner at the Club Hotel followed in the evening".

The Second Test was at Sydney on June 28th and the teams were:- England: J. Sullivan, S. Rix, T. Howley, C. Carr, F. Evans, F. Gallagher and J. Parkin (capt.), W. Cunliffe, J. Bennett, W. Burgess, J. Darwell, A. Brough and J. Thompson. Australia: Fravenfelder, Horder, Craig (capt.), Gorman, Aynsley, Hunt and Thompson, Bennett, Watt, Potter, Armbruster, O'Connor (Ives) and Latta. Loose forward Frank Gallagher had to play stand off and skipper Jonty Parkin, hardly able to walk on damaged ankles, was told by manager Harry Dannatt to "go out there and try running". This he did and scored a try! Sullivan kicked a goal and the Lions had won 5-3 and retained the Ashes before a crowd of 33,842. In a letter to the Hull Evening News, Harold described the game as "the most exciting I have ever seen. Three minutes from time Australia were leading 3-0 and pressing on our line when Parkin broke away, kicked ahead and dived to score fifteen yards from the posts. Sullivan took great care with the kick and landed the ball over the bar. Everyone went mad for a few minutes". It had been a great game. Darwell and Bennett played splendidly.

The following day the New South Wales R.L. took the tourists on a trip round the beautiful Sydney Harbour area and then the day after up to Queensland for the remaining matches.

"The trip round Sydney Harbour was magnificent. Called at Killarney for lunch, then onto the Zoological Gardens at Taronga Park. Left Sydney at 7 p.m. on the Monday via Northern Rivers to play a match at Lismore where we arrived at 7.30 p.m. on the Tuesday. We were given a civic reception by the Lord Mayor, Ald. R. Brewster, and so big were the crowds we couldn't get into the reception at first. The interest in our visits to country towns is surprising. A crowd of 8,000 turned out to see us. The new Gordon Stand was soon booked up. Carr had a hand in all five tries scored by Ring. Bentham scored the other try in only his second game of the tour due to injury. Bert Gilbert was coach to the North Coast side. We won an entertaining match 28-19.

In the evening a banquet was given to us by the Far North Coast R.L. Association at the Diggers Picture Theatre. Many prominent men were present, including Mr. E. Briscombe (President of the Association), Mr. R. Best (President of the Lower River Football League) and Mr. Gordon. The Lismore Philharmonic Male Chorus gave a concert. There were sixteen toasts at the banquet!

We left Lismore at 7 a.m. the next day for Brisbane, where we arrived at dinner-time. Beautiful scenery along the Tweed River. We are staying at the Hotel Daniel again. Two hours after our arrival, fifteen players set off for the hundred mile trip to Rockhampton where we beat a Central Queensland side 34-2 before a crowd of

Civic Reception given to the English Rugby League Team in Sydney on May 28th.

Back row: J. C. Clayton, A. Clayton, T. Phelan.
Second row: Mr. Pullein, J. T. Harvey, C. Pollard, B. Gronow, D. Murray (Trainer), C. Carr, D. Hurcombe, W. Bentham, J. Bennett, J. Price, R. Fusedale.
Third row: Mr. Collier, Mr. Watson, H. Bowman, B. Sloman, A. Brough, S. Whitty, S. Rix, J. Darwell, J. Thompson, J. Burgess, E. Knapman, J. Sullivan, J. Bacon, Mr. Brown, R. Clayton, W. G. Layton, Alderman Bramston, Mr. Stevenson (Mayor of Ipswich).
Fourth row: J. Quinlan, W. Fillan, S. G. Ball, E. O. Osborne, J. H. Dannatt, Alderman Gilpin (Lord Mayor), Sir George Fuller (Premier), C. W. Oakes (Chief Secretary), F. Flowers M.L.C. (Patron of the New South Wales Eugby League), J. Dooley M.L.A., G. Cann M.L.A., F. Delaney.
Front row: W. J. Chaseling, R. Savage, F. Mooney, F. Gallagher, D. Rees, W. Lennon, J. Parkin (Captain), J. Ring, T. Howley, F. Evans, C. M. Dougall.

English Rugby League Team.

Back row: D. Hurcombe, E. Knapman, J. Bennett, S. Rix, J. Price, W. Cunliffe, W. Bentham, A. Brough.
Second row: C. A. Pollard, J. T. Thompson, J. Sullivan, W. Burgess, R. Sloman, J. Darwell, H. Bowman, B. Gronow, J. Ring.
Third tow: W. H. Pullein, C. W. Carr, S. Whitty, E. Osborne, J. Parkin, J. H. Dannatt, J. A. Bacon, F. Gallagher, J. Watson.
Front row: W. Fillan, D. Rees, W. Mooney, D. Murray, T. Howley, F. Evans, J. T. Harvey.

Right:
Harold outside the Hotel Brighton.

Below:
Hotel Brighton, Brighton-le-Sands, New South Wales - Australia.

8,000 on Saturday 5th July. Admission prices were: Ground 2s-2d. (11p), Grandstand 4s/4d. (22p), Children 9d. (4p), Programme was 6d. (2$\frac{1}{2}$p). JULY 8th. Beat Maryborough 22-3 and then enjoyed a banquet at the Royal Hotel".

The third and final Test Match was played at the Exhibition Ground in Brisbane on July 12th. The teams were:- England: J. Sullivan, S. Rix, T. Howley, J. Bacon, F. Evans, D. Hurcombe and J. Parkin (capt.), W. Cunliffe, J. Bennett, W. Burgess, J. Darwell, J. Price and F. Gallagher. Australia: Fravenfelder, Paton, Craig (capt.), Gorman, Aynsley, Hunt and Thompson, Bennett, Watt, Potter, Armbuster, O'Connor (Oxford) and Latta. His Excellency, The Governor, Sir Matthew Nathan, kicked off. A crowd of 36,000 paid £3,315 to see Australia win back some pride by being successful 21-11. Frank Gallagher became the first Lion to be sent off in a Test Match down under. "WEDNESDAY JULY 16th. The final match of our Australia tour. We beat the Combined Australia Universities at Sydney 31-13 but were behind 8-13 well into the second half before our heavier forwards took over.

Our record was played 18, won 14, lost 4, points for 466, points against 258. Around 320,000 watched the matches and paid £25,000, ensuring the financial success of the tour. Queensland and Brisbane have made great strides since the last tour in 1920 but support has fallen away in Sydney, probably because officials of the Cricket Ground have retained another stand for their members which has penalised the League and the tourists financially".

The party left for New Zealand on 17th July without any intimation of the number of matches to be played there. The New South Wales R.L. general committee entertained the tourists to a banquet and theatre party as an official farewell.

The party left Sydney for Wellington on the T.S.S. "Manuka" on July 21st, the birthday of Mr. Finan. "Arrived 22nd July. Heard that Johnny Weismuller (later of Tarzan fame), had won the 100m swimming semi-final in the Paris Olympics. The first game in New Zealand was against a strong South Auckland side at Hamilton when we combined well to win 28-16. The next match was harder when an Auckland representatives side were beaten 24-11 but Cunliffe was sent off. A crowd of 19,000 watched the match".

Skipper Jonty Parkin and Jim Sullivan went down with diptheria and there was some talk of quarantining the whole party which didn't materialise.

"JULY 28th. Lower Walkato were beaten 30-12, played at Ngaruawatria before a crowd of 2,000, we made many openings. JULY 30th. Beat Auckland Province 28-13. AUGUST 2nd. Parkin, Sullivan, Bacon, Carr, Pollard, Ring, Whitty, Bowman and Hurcombe were absent through injury and illness for the First Test against New Zealand at Auckland". Playing for the first time in their white strip with red and blue 'V', the Tourists had Bill Cunliffe sent off for the second time in New Zealand. A crowd of 22,000 saw a hard game in muddy conditions and despite tries from Bentham and Thompson and a goal from Thompson, the Tourists went down 8-16.

AUGUST 6th. Weakened again, England went down in the Second Test at Wellington 11-13 before a crowd of 4,000. They led 11-0 at half-time through tries from Rix, Carr and Howley with a goal from Thompson but a converted try in the last minute gave New Zealand the rubber. AUGUST 9th. The Third Test Match in a week was played at Dunedin before a crowd of 14,000 when England fielded a more representative side including Harold Bowman. Superior speed and cleverness gave the Tourists a 31-18 victory with tries from Hurcombe, Brough (2), Price, Evans, Howley and Carr while Sullivan kicked five goals.

Further victories were gained over West Coast at Greymouth 65-8 and over Canterbury 47-10 before a crowd of 9,000 at Christchurch. Nine matches had been played in just three weeks, an incredible feat. Seven matches were won and two lost. Points for 272 and 117 points against.

During their visit to New Zealand, the hospitality given to the touring side was overwhelming. The Hinemoa Maori Entertainers gave a grand concert, the Metropolitan Trotting Club entertained the party and especially good was the Football League's Smoke Social in the Embassy Salon, Moray Place was memorable. Sightseeing trips to Rotorua, Wairakei, Waingaro, Hot Spring's and Toupo were very enjoyable. At various times on the tour, the Tourists were entertained by Milne and Choyce, the Auckland Orphans Club, the Commercial Travellers Club and the New Zealand Rugby League Council.

Of the twenty seven games played on tour, prop. Bill Burgess played in twenty two and centre Tommy Howley played in twenty one. Jim Sullivan broke the tour record for goals with eighty four while winger Johnny Ring was leading try scorer with twenty three. Harold Bowman played in fourteen matches and scored eight tries while Stan Whitty also played fourteen times and scored five tries. Record receipts of more than £30,000 ensured the financial success of the tour.

The party left Wellington on August 23rd on the R.M.S. "Tahiti" and called in at Raratonga and Papete en route to San Francisco where they arrived on September 5th, staying at the Hotel Stewart.

A thirty mile motor tour of the city and suburbs impressed the Tourists but all they really wanted was to get home to England. The party moved onto Chicago by train, a three day trip. They toured Armours Packing Plant works and stockyard and left after just six hours in the "Windy City", arriving at Niagara on September 10th for a nine hour stay during which the party visited the great Gorge.

They arrived at the Hotel Earle in New York at 7.15 a.m. on September 11th and spent two days sightseeing, notably the Brooklyn Bridge and a short steamer trip around Manhattan Island, before leaving on September 13th on the S.S. "Baltic", arriving in Liverpool eight days later, via Cobb (Queenstown) and dispersal home by train.

Unfortunately, Harold did not appear to keep a diary on the trip home, but from shipping records we do know daily meal times were Breakfast - 8 p.m., Lunch - 1p p.m., Dinner - 7 p.m. Deck Chair hire was £1/10- (£1.50) per day. A shave cost 9d. (4p), haircut 11d. - (5p), shampoo 9d. (4p), wireless mesages could be sent for 10d. (4p) per word. The tour had lasted five months.

A complimentary dinner for the Touring party was held at the Griffin Hotel in Leeds on Thursday October 2nd when Mr. Dannatt, Mr. Osborne, Mr. J. B. Cooke and Mr. J. F. Whitaker, supported by Jonty Parkin, gave toasts to "The King", "The Tourists" and "Rugby Football League".

Official Third Test Match Programme.

(Left to right): Harold, Jack Price, Ben Gronow, Frank Gallagher, Jim Sullivan, Danny Hurcombe.

Harold (left) and Stan Whitty (right) enjoying a day out.

Deck games on board the "Manuka".

Unique Maori entertainment was offered in the Kimi Hall, Ngarnowakia.

Right: Maori Ladies.

BRENTS LTD., BATHGATE HOUSE, ROTORUA.

Covers 2 Acres   All on One Floor   Capacity 250   Spacious Dancing Hall
Lounges and Drawing Rooms   Adjoining Sanatorium Grounds and Bath Entrance
Electric Light   Unlimited Hot Water Service   THE One Place to Stay
TELEGRAMS: "BRENTS," ROTORUA.

Described as the "Wonderland of New Zealand", Rotorua offered golf and tennis all year round, boating, fishing, geysers and hot springs, boiling cauldrons and mud pools.

1924 TOUR

MATCH RESULTS:

IN AUSTRALIA

Victoria (Melbourne)	won	45-13	15,000
Southern District (Cootamundra)	won	31-4	
Newcastle (Newcastle)	won	43-18	
New England (Tamworth)	won	34-17	
New South Wales (Sydney)	won	10-5	41,657
New South Wales (Sydney)	lost	18-33	37,000
Ipswich (Ipswich)	won	17-0	
Queensland (Brisbane)	lost	10-25	40,000
Toowoomba (Toowoomba)	lost	20-23	10,000
New South Wales (Sydney)	won	43-5	26,042
AUSTRALIA (Sydney)	**won**	**22-3**	**50,000**
Orange (Orange)	won	42-23	
AUSTRALIA (Sydney)	**won**	**5-3**	**33,842**
North Coast (Lismore)	won	28-19	8,000
Central Queensland (Rockhampton)	won	34-20	8,000
Maryborough (Maryborough)	won	22-3	
AUSTRALIA (Brisbane)	**lost**	**11-21**	**36,000**
Universities (Sydney)	won	31-23	

SUMMARY:
Played 18   Won 14   Lost 4
For
Tries 104   Goals 77   Points 466
Against
Tries 56   Goals 45   Points 258
Won Test series 2-1

IN NEW ZEALAND

South Auckland (Hamilton)	won	28-16	
Auckland (Auckland)	won	24-11	19,000
Lower Waikato (Ngarnowakia)	won	30-12	
Auckland Province (Auckland)	won	28-13	
NEW ZEALAND (Auckland)	**lost**	**8-16**	**22,000**
NEW ZEALAND (Wellington)	**lost**	**11-13**	**6,000**
NEW ZEALAND (Dunedin)	**won**	**31-18**	**14,000**
West Coast (Greymouth)	won	65-8	
Canterbury (Christchurch)	won	47-10	9,000

SUMMARY:
Played 9   Won 7   Lost 2
For
Tries 64   Goals 40   Points 272
Against
Tries 25   Goals 21   Points 117
Lost Test series 2-1

TOUR TOTALS
Played 27   Won 21   Lost 6
For
Tries 168   Goals 177   Points 738
Against
Tries 81   Goals 66   Points 375

TOUR PARTY:

Managers: J. H. Dannatt (Hull) and E. Osborne (Warrington)
Captain: J. Parkin (Wakefield T.)
Trainer: D. Murray

	App	Tries	Gls	Pts
J. Bacon (Leeds)	8	2	0	6
J. Bennett (Rochdale H.)	19	2	0	6
W. Bentham (Broughton R.)	7	7	0	21
H. Bowman (Hull)	14	8	0	24
A. Brough (Oldham)	12	14	1	44
W. Burgess (Barrow)	22	3	1	11
C. Carr (Barrow)	17	9	0	27
W. Cunliffe (Warrington0	17	3	0	9
J. Darwell (Leigh)	15	5	0	15
F. Evans (Swinton)	14	13	0	39
F. Gallagher (Batley)	16	3	0	9
B. Gronow (Huddersfield)	8	1	5	13
T. Howley (Wigan)	21	13	0	39
D. Hurcombe (Wigan)	11	5	0	15
E. Knapman (Oldham)	11	0	1	2
W. Mooney (Leigh)	12	0	1	2
J. Parkin (Wakefield T.)	13	13	6	51
C. Pollard (Wakefield T.)	9	6	1	20
J. Price (Wigan)	9	8	0	24
D. Rees (Halifax)	12	2	0	6
J. Ring (Wigan)	15	23	0	69
S. Rix (Oldham)	17	17	0	51
R. Sloman (Oldham)	3	0	0	0
J. Sullivan (Wigan)	17	0	84	168
J. Thompson (Leeds)	18	6	17	52
S. Whitty (Hull)	14	5	0	15

Rochdale H. v. Hull
2nd Round 1928

Gangway

Gangway!
Harold (right) bursts through in
a second round cup tie against
Rochdale Hornets in 1928.

Harold scores one of his 75 tries
for Hull F.C.

(Picture courtesy Hull Daily Mail)

28

FOUR YEARS ON

After a trial match at Rochdale on 27th February 1928, the Tour party for Australia and New Zealand was announced. Jonty Parkin (Wakefield Trinity) was tour captain for the second time and became the first player to make three tours. Frank Gallagher (Leeds) was selected but withdrew to be replaced by his Leeds team mate Joe Thompson. Swinton players Bryn and Jack Evans became the first brothers to tour.

The party was:-

Managers: G. F. Hutchins (Oldham) and E. Osborne (Warrington). Trainer:- D. Murray.

J. Parkin (Wakefield Trinity), T. Askin (Featherstone Rovers), N. Bentham (Wigan Highfield), F. Bowen (St. Helens Rec), H. Bowman (Hull), J. Brough (Leeds), W. Burgess (Barrow), O. Dolan (St. Helens Rec), A. Ellaby (St. Helens), B. Evans (Swinton), J. Evans (Swinton), L. Fairclough (St. Helens), A. Fildes (St. Helens Rec), A. Frodsham (St. Helens), W. Gowers (Rochdale Hornets), T. E. Gwynne (Hull), B. Halfpenny (St. Helens), W. Horton (Wakefield Trinity), J. Oliver (Batley), W. Rees (Swinton), M. Rosser (Leeds), R. Sloman (Oldham), J. Sullivan (Wigan), J. Thompson (Leeds), W. Williams (Salford) and H. Young (Bradford Northern) plus T. D. Watson and W. H. Pellein.

Harold's selection raised some eyebrows outside the Hull area but on his Hull form it was a deserved honour.

John Wilson, Secretary to the Rugby Football League, sent confirmation of the tour itinerary to Harold on April 17th. He was to share berth 223 with Emlyn Gwynne, his Hull team-mate, on the S.S. Cathay. It was the fifth tour to Australia and New Zealand made by the Rugby Football League.

The party left St. Pancras station at 9.55 a.m. on April 20th for Tilbury Docks and the P & O ship S.S. Cathay, under the command of Commander W. F. Cossey, R.N.R. A Sports and Amusements Programme was set up under the Chairman, Mr. E. Osborne, assisted by Mr. T. Watson (Secretary) and Mr. T. Pullein (Treasurer) together with committee members Sullivan, Rosser and Parkin.

The itinerary was scheduled to be:-

April 25th - Algiers, April 27th - Marseille, April 30th - Port Said, May 3rd - Port Sudan, May 5th - Aden, May 12th - Colombo, May 22nd - Fremantle, May 26th - Adelaide, May 28th - Melbourne. Altogether, a six week trip. Deck games, whist drives, fancy dress parties, dances, treasure hunts, cricket matches and various competitions helped to pass time with quite a bit of training included as well!

Harold's dad wrote to him onboard, hoping he'd got his sea legs by now and didn't he think Blackburn Rovers were playing well. A Mr. Ridley asked if Harold would get him a couple of long team photographs and one of the Sydney Cricket ground.

"The trip reached Fremantle May 21st and the team were quite excited and went ashore at 7 p.m. and toured the city of Perth before returning to the 'Cathay' and the trip across the Bight, past Kangeroo Island, to Adelaide where we had our first practice match at 7 a.m. and then the party were guests of the Racecourse company where we were most impressed when the crowd stood bare headed for the National Anthem. Then onto the Adelaide Oval where we saw an Australian Rules Match. Their players have to be very fit. Mr. Kirkwood of the Australian Rugby Union welcomed us. "We care not whether you are amateurs or professionals, you represent a good sport and you are from the mother country and we are delighted to meet you and wish you success on your tour". Mr. Marlow, Secretary of the South Australian Rugby Union, also welcomed us and bid us to "come and sup". It made us reflect on our treatment by the Rugby Union at home. They are a find sporting lot out here with no room for snobbishness. The Adelaide soccer club also made us most welcome together with the cricket club. None of the codes had anything in common with ours and yet they showed us great courtesy. A Mr. Kurlow had travelled 1,200 miles from Queensland to officially greet us.

The official cable of welcome was received on board and read "we hope you have an enjoyable trip and all your party are fit. Tremendous public interest in your tour. May the best side win". - Miller, Hon. Sec., Australian Rugby League. The Bishop of Adelaide is the Right Rev. Nutter-Thomas, formerly a curate at Wakefield Cathedral. We arrived at Melbourne and some of the party left the ship to play a match at Cootamundra on May 30th while the rest of the party travelled by ship to Sydney. Before leaving Melbourne, the ship's Commander and Purser agreed to be photographed with the team after Sundays Divine Service which provided the passengers with a fine opportunity for a snap".

The team selected to play against South Western District (Group IX) was:- Sullivan, Ellaby, Oliver, Frodsham, Brough, Parkin (capt.) and Fairclough, Burgess, Bentham and Bowman, Sloman,

Fildes and Young. Travelling reserves:- Gwynne and Young.

A crowd of 8,000 saw the local side play well above themselves and they gained a 14-14 draw. Right on time, Harold Bowman was sent off. One local newspaper reported it was for kicking the opposition No.10 Torphy who "reeled from the scrum, blood streaming from his mouth and collapsed". However, the referee's report indicated the sending off was for striking. In a letter home to his parents, Harold explained Torphy had been pulling and pushing him all the match and his patience finally ran out and he hit him. Harold later appeared before the local League and he was cautioned. The South Western Rugby League (Group Nine) gave an official dinner at the Albion Hotel after the match. Toasts were made to The King, The Tourists, The Maryborough Rugby League, Queensland Rugby League, Wide Bay and Burnett Rugby League and the Referees Association. The team left by the Temora Mail train next day at 7.15 p.m., arriving at their Sydney headquarters, The Doncaster Hotel, at 5.30 a.m. on Thursday May 31st.

"We all enjoyed a steamer trip of about sixty miles from Fort Macquaire, including all the wonderful sights of Sydney Harbour.

A crowd of 55,000 at the Sydney Cricket Ground on Saturday June 2nd saw us lose to New South Wales 15-20 in an exciting game. Thompson, Ellaby and J. Evans scored tries and Gowers converted them all. Ellaby was the outstanding player on the field and he was well supported by Gwynne and Dolan".

Two days later the Tourists turned the tables, beating New South Wales 22-9 before another crowd of 48,000. A very fast game with deadly tackling saw Ellaby (2), Parkin, Horton score tries and Sullivan kick five goals. Sir Joynton Smith, Chairman of the Australian Board of Control, gave a party after the match which was talked about for days after. In the third match, New South Wales gained another victory, this time 22-7. A crowd of 38,000 meant that the tourists had already been watched by 149,000 people in four matches in nine days. Parkin and Dolan had fractures of their thumbs and missed the match. Good performances from Bowman, Rees, J. Evans and Fildes.

"The party received a reception at the Tattershall Club, a very exclusive club where we have been made honorary members during our stay in Sydney. What a magnificent building it is.

Situated in Elizabeth Street, it was opened on 27th September 1927 and has a barber's shop, bars, card room, lounge, lending library, telephone bureau plus a superb swimming pool on the third floor with seating accommodation there for 300. Our two managers were entertained to lunch by Mr. Dick Wooton, proprietor of the hotel where we are staying and a famous racehorse owner and trainer well known at home. The team laid a wreath on the Cenotaph in St. Martin's Place and then we met the great cricketers J. T. Gregory and

Harold and Emlyn Gwynne at the Boulevard.

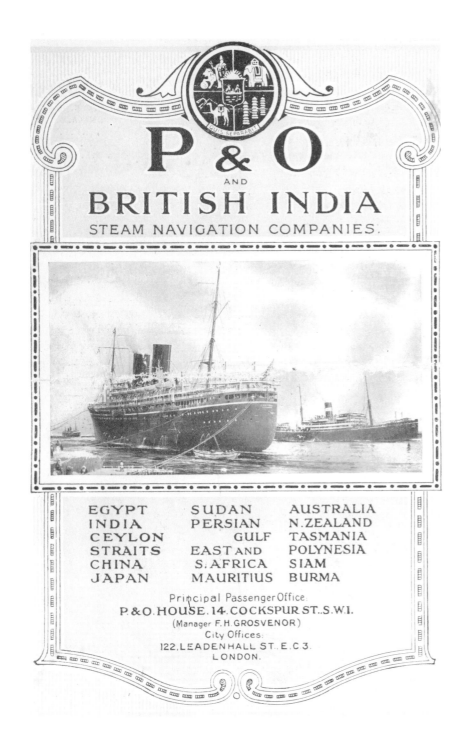

*Harold (right) and Emlyn Gwynne
wearing the official tour uniform
on board the 'Cathay'.*

Cover of the official ship's passenger list.

T. E. Mailey who are looking forward to the visit of the English cricketers next season. Mr. Osborne and Jonty Parkin had a flight around Sydney, even looping the loop!

Scrimmaging is still a source of concern as we are being penalised too often for our own good and we had a long and amicable meeting with local referees in an attempt to sort things out.

WEDNESDAY JUNE 13th. Beat the Far Northern Coast 20-9 at the Lismore Rec. before a crowd of 6,500. Before the match, two curtain-raisers were staged, Byron Juniors v High School and North Lismore v Marist Brothers. The Far Northern Rugby League's Association entertained us to a dinner after the match at the Freemasons Hotel, chaired by the Chairman, Capt. L. M. Gordon. After the dinner, most of us attended a Jazz cabaret at the Appollo Hall".

Harold's wife wrote to him enclosing a photograph of his sons, George and Sydney (Keith), just one week old.

The Tourists lost their third match of the Tour when they went down 7-21 to Queensland at the Exhibition Ground, Brisbane on June 16th. Burgess, leading the side in the continued absence of Parkin, was sent off for fighting, the crowd of 25,000 hooting. The home team won the scrums and combined well against some weak tackling. Four days later Ipswich were beaten 23-13 at Brisbane before a crowd of 2,000. Showing greatly improved form, especially in the first half, the Tourists scored tries through Frodsham, Gwynne,

Halfpenny (2) and Horton with Sullivan kicking four goals. After the match the Ipswich Rugby League entertained the Tourists at Bearkleys Cafe.

Just three days later came the main business of the tour, the Test Match at Brisbane. England's side was:- Sullivan (capt.), Askin, Oliver, Brough, Ellaby, Fairclough and Rees, Burgess, Bentham, Bowman, Fildes, Sloman and Horton. Australia wore gum green and wattle gold jerseys with the Australian Coat of Arms for the first time. On their side were Craig, Aynsley, Gorman (Capt.), Hardy, Freestone, Laws and Edwards, Steinohrt, Justice, York, Dempsey, Treweeke and Armbruster. The Tourists objected to the appointment of referee Leighton and C. Broadfoot refereed the match. A crowd of 39,000 saw the game and paid £4,348. The game slipped out of Australia's hands in the first twenty minutes when a clever dummy from Billo Rees (scrum half with Jonty Parkin out with a broken thumb) fooled the whole Australian back line and put Horton in for a try to add to a penalty goal from Sullivan and a Fairclough try. From that brilliant start, England gained a famous 15-12 victory with another try from Ellaby and two goals from Sullivan. The Brisbane Sunday Mail headline was "The rose of England blooms again! The Homeland's sons taught Australia a sound, and it's hoped a salutary lesson. They outclassed us in weight, skill, brains and speed more than the score suggests". Joe Oliver, Fairclough and

Enjoying a dip in the Cathay's luxurious(!) swimming pool.
These pictures and the following seven are courtesy of Alf Ellaby.

Passing through the Suez Canal.

The harbour at Aden.

Natives at Aden rowed out to the 'Cathay' selling goods.

Impressive buildings at Port Sudan.

Rees had magnificent games and Bob Sloman played a stormer. One of his opponents recognised this fact after the match and said he didn't know how Bob had stood up to such a hammering. Sloman replied he never felt a thing as he was slightly deaf!

After a night of celebration, most of the team left next morning for the long trip to Rockhampton to play Central Queensland. The Tourists were victorious 27-11 before a crowd of 10,000. A local show and a racing carnival meant accommodation was scarce and the team slept in what could only be described as a cowshed. Then it was onto Townsville, another long journey taking over twenty hours. It was the first match between an English team and a side drawn from Northern Queensland. 11,000 people paid £1,076 to see the Tourists win their third match in a week by 30-16.

There followed a grand evening at Buchanans Hotel and then a visit to the Wintergarden Theatre. Sunday the team were guests at League Football and on the Monday they were taken on a tour of the Ross River Meat works and a trip to Magnetic Island before catching the 9 p.m. train back to Brisbane. Visits to the Wool Auction, to a boot manufacturing company and various motor trips brought the team's visit to Brisbane nearly to a close. They had received tremendous hospitality.

Captain Bert Hinkler, the record breaking England to Australia Flyer, kicked off the next game when the Tourists met Wide Bay, Bundaberg. A crowd of 4,000 saw Harold Young score a hat-trick of tries in England's runaway 61-13 win. "JULY 6th. Rise and shine at 5.30 a.m. and then off by train to Toowoomba, 2,800 ft. above sea level. We all wore our overcoats. A large crowd greeted us at the Town Hall reception when the Mayor made a witty speech, reminding his audience of how many hats were lost when Toowoomba beat us in 1924. Mr. Fred Hutchin got one back in his speech when he said he had heard the first hat thrown in the air was that of the referee. Such was the interest in the match that the town of Charlesville, three hundred and eighty miles away, closed all business premises for the weekend for people to come to the ground. Their town's football team played Gundiwindi before our match. Toowoomba had never lost a match on the Sports Oval, but we beat them 17-12 before a crowd of 12,000. Jack Evans underwent an operation for appendicitis in Sydney". JULY 11th. Dolan and Bowman were sent off in a rough match against Newcastle. Harold reckoned the referee was unsure who committed the foul so he sent off both of them. The Tourists won 19-17 before a crowd of 7,000 who paid £580.

The second Test Match was played on the Sydney Cricket Ground on July 14th before a crowd of 44,548. Parkin played with his thumb broken in two places five weeks earlier hardly mended but the plucky Wakefield player had it broken again at the beginning of the second half and he was to miss the rest of the tour.

The teams were: England - Sullivan, Askin, Oliver, Brough, Ellaby, Rees, Parkin (Capt.), Burgess, Bentham, Thompson, Fildes, Sloman and Horton. Australia - Hardy, Byrne, Gorman (Capt.), Craig, Maher, Weissel, Busch, Steinohrt, Justice, York, Dempsey, Treweeke and Armbruster.

The Australians made five changes from their team in the First Test including a new half-back pairing.

Harold Bowman was not available for selection.

Played in a quagmire, England won 8-0 with tries from Ellaby and Parkin and a goal from Sullivan. The match was refereed by L. Deane. The Tourists won the cup presented by the Sydney Tattersall's Club for competition between England and Australia, played for the first time on this tour.

A tour of the Parkes district was undertaken on Tuesday July 17th and included a Ball in the Parkes Picture Palace, a Banquet in the Protestant Hall and a Banquet in aid of the Parkes Hospital, a visit to Forbes and a reception by their Mayor, Ald. Twogood. A Jacaranda Ovalifolia tree was planted at the entrance to Parkes High School to mark the Tourist's visit, after visits to the bush.

WEDNESDAY 18th JULY. A crowd of 9,000 were at the match against Western New South Wales at Parkes which England won comfortably 22-9. A record 32 toasts were proposed at the after match dinner!

The Third Test was played at the Sydney Cricket Ground on Saturday July 21st before a crowd of 37,000. A full week's special training made all the difference to the Australians' performance. Referee Lal Deane, brother of an Australian player associated with the Oldham Club some years previous, allowed a try which the England players claimed was a knock-on but generally the Tourists performance was under-par. Australia won 21-14. Fairclough (two tries) and Sullivan (four goals) were England's points scorers. The England team was: Sullivan, Gwynne, Oliver, Askin, Ellaby, Fairclough and Rees, Burgess, Bentham, Bowman, Fildes, Sloman and Horton. Australia: Hardy, Wearing, Gorman (capt.), Craig, Pearce, Weissel, Busch, Steinohrt, Justice, Kingston, Dempsey, Treweeke and Armbruster.

"Spent full day at Taronga Park Zoo at the invitation of the Hon. Fred Flowers, a trustee and builder of some wonderful outdoor Zoological Gardens and then on the Monday we were entertained by Mr. J. Davis at the "Sydney Referee". Mr. Davis writes for the paper under the nom-de-plume of "The Cynic" and he presented each of us with a magnificent bronze medallion, suitably inscribed.

Attended a farewell dinner on our behalf at Sargeants Cafe in the market street and then a Theatre Party at St. James Theatre ("Rio Rita")".

The financial returns in Australia were encouraging and of

Natives selling goods on the quay at Algiers.

Avoiding sun stroke on board the 'Cathay'.

English Rugby League Team.

Back row: N. Bentham, A. Ellaby, H. Bowman, J. F. Thompson, H. O. Dolan, W. A. Williams, J. Brough.
Second row: E. J. Evans, R. Sloman, H. Young, A. Fildes, W. Burgess, W. Horton, J. Sullivan, B. Halfpenny.
Third row: F. Bowen, J. Oliver, A. Frodsham, G. F. Hutchins, J. Parkin, E. Osborne, T. E. Gwynne, W. Gowers, M. A. Rosser.
Front row: B. Evans, L. Fairclough, D. Murray, T. Askin, W. Rees.

"Having a spell" after training in Sydney.

(Photograph courtesy Alf Ellaby).

Harold (left), Jim Sullivan (second left) and Jim Brough (right) enjoy a day at the races.

greenstone hearts inscribed in gold with a Kiwi, for their respective wives.

Mr. Osborne observed that no rain had fallen during any of their matches. "We have seen the eternal snow of the Southern Alps and at Bluff, the most southerly gas lamp in the world. Financially, it has been the most successful tour ever made by an English Rugby League side and as far as I know, the first English team which has won the Ashes in both of these countries on a tour".

Both countries were growing very strong in the game.

Mr. Hutchins advised the New Zealanders to concentrate on physical fitness and to place less importance on defence. He considered that Auckland had one of the greatest sporting publics in the world.

Mr. Osborne also paid tribute to the great enthusiasm shown everywhere they went. He was particularly impressed with the beauty of the Buller and Otira Gorges. Harold confessed he would have loved to settle in New Zealand.

Looking back in later years, that great winger Alf Ellaby recalled "the 1928 side is now referred to as one of the great sides but when the team was chosen the press gave us no chance and thought that there were only six players of Test class in the party. Poor diet and training on board ship left us in poor shape for the start of the tour and we won only two of the first six games. Fortunately, we were able to re-organise our training and tactics and win the Ashes in Australia and New Zealand".

Nearly 500,000 people had watched the twenty four matches played, of which eighteen were won, one drawn and five lost. Five hundred and fifty eight points were scored and two hundred and ninety one conceded. Harold Bowman played in 14 of the matches scoring 2 tries while Emlyn Gwynne scored 7 tries in 11 games. Sullivan kicked 52 goals. Alf Ellaby scored 20 tries while Frodsham touched down 15 times. Jack Evans and Jonty Parkin made only 3 and 4 appearances respectively through injury. Billo Rees only missed 5 games on tour.

"AUGUST 28th. Left Auckland by S.S. Niagara via Suva (Fiji) and Honolulu for Vancouver. SEPTEMBER 14th. Arrived at Vancouver where we stayed at the Vancouver Hotel. Sightseeing by auto to Stanley Park, the Harding Memorial (where President Harding gave his last address), West End residential district and Oriental sections". Two exhibition games were played in Canada. Bowman, Frodsham, Dolan, Halfpenny, Young and B. Evans guested for Wales in their 30-17 defeat by England. Ellaby, Brough (2), Oliver, Askin, Parkin, Bowen and Horton scored tries. Oliver (2) and Parkin kicked goals. For Wales Sullivan kicked 4 goals and Gwynne, Frodsham, and Rees scored tries. "After-match reception in the hotel's Meraloma Club. Next day left by the C.P.R. train "Trans-

TATTERSALL'S CLUB
ELIZABETH STREET
SYDNEY

Canada" at 6.30 p.m., arriving at Toronto on September 19th at 8.40 a.m. and then onto Niagara Falls. What a sight! Saw the "Home of Shredded Wheat" factory and then left for Toronto, left there at 11 p.m. and arrived at Montreal at 8 a.m. next day. Stayed at the Windsor Hotel".

The same two sides played a second match, England winning 21-17 with tries from Askin (3), Ellaby and Bentham and 3 goals from Joe Oliver. Gwynne, Rosser, and Frodsham were try scorers for Wales and Jim Sullivan kicked another 4 goals. Mr. Hutchins refereed both games. Jim Brough recalled "Although it was the end of a long, hard and successful tour, the two games were far from friendly with players still wanting to prove a point as to who should have been in the Test side".

Final diary notes were "SEPTEMBER 21st. Left Montreal by S.S. Duchess of Atholl en route for Liverpool. I shared a cabin with

Gowers, Bentham and Gwynne. The ship was in charge of Commander G. Hamilton. Bugle sounded 30 minutes before dinner. Lights out at 11 p.m. in the Dining Room and midnight in the Lounge and Smoking Room. Bar closed at 11 p.m. An orchestra played at lunch, dinner and afternoon tea. Smoking was permitted in the dining saloon 45 minutes after lunch and dinner but not after breakfast.

Members of the side gave rousing choruses at several concerts in the lounge organised by the passengers in aid of Seamen's Charities. SEPTEMBER 28th. Arrived at Liverpool and dispersed home by train."

A 'Welcome Home' dinner was given to the Tourists by the Rugby Football League at the Midland Hotel in Manchester on October 17th when each member of the touring party received a bonus of £136.00.

In a rush towards England's goal, Bailey (N.S.W.) is upended.

Wearing, the N.S.W. wing three-quarter, is well tackled by Bryn Evans (England). Rosser (England) is racing to his assistance and Ellaby (No. 7) is standing by. Behind Wearing, Hardy and Bailey, of the N.S.W. team. Sprawled on the ground in the rear is Brien, the N.S.W. five-eighth.

England v. New South Wales at the Cricket Ground, Sydney. England won by 22 points to 9. Harry Cavanough with the ball is fending off Bowman (left), but Horton (England) seems to have his measure. Kingston, at the rear awaits developments

A Valiant Effort to Smother A Kick

One of the many thrills of the international Rugby League game yesterday was the valiant effort by Busch (the N.S.W. half-back) to knock down a kick by Bryn Evans (England). He has worked round from behind the scrum.

Tearing Rushes Helped N.S.W.'s Win

Yorke, the N.S.W. front row forward, tears his way through a breaking ruck. He has pushed Bryn Evans (England) to one side, in his eagerness to get to the ball, which, however, has been pounced on by Halfpenny, the English lock-forward.

Treweeke (the N.S.W. forward) was everywhere,
and came out on top in this episode.

Fi! Fi! Fo! Fum! I Smell The Blood . . .

Paddy Maher, the N.S.W. captain, sits on the face of an Englishman
while the ball goes away to Bowman (England).

Harold (far right) and six of his colleagues enjoy a rest after training in Brisbane.

(Photograph courtesy Alf Ellaby).

The Australian Rugby League Team.

In front: A. Edwards (Q.).

Second row (left to right):
E. Freestone (N.S.W.), E. Mead (selector),
T. Gorman (Q., captain), A. Burdon
(selector and coach), C. Yorke (N.S.W.).

Third row :
H. Sunderland (secretary Q.R.L.),
V. Armbruster (Q.), G. Treweeke (N.S.W.),
H. Steinohrt (Q.), D. Dempsey (Q.),
H. Flegg (selector).

Back row:
A. Justice (N.S.W.), F. Laws (Q.),
C. Aynsley (Q.), N. Hardy (N.S.W.),
J. Craig (Q.).

Twenty two members of the tour party enjoy a day in the open air baths.
Harold is at the back of the group.

First Test in Brisbane.
Bowman dribbles through with Horton on his left and Burgess on his right in front of referee Broadfoot.
Australians from left to right are Laws, Dempsey and York.

Right:
Mr. Osborne, Jim Sullivan, Dally Messenger
and Tom Gorman before the First Test.

50

*Captain Bert Hinkler shows two of
the tourists his aeroplane.*

(Photograph courtesy Alf Ellaby).

*Harold (right) walks away after being
sent off against Newcastle.*

A crowd of 37,000 packed into the Sydney Cricket Ground for the Third Test.

(Photograph courtesy Alf Ellaby).

Harold (second left) in action, possibly the Third Test.

League Touring Team Leaders.

From left to right: Messrs. F. Hutchins (secretary and manager), J. Parkin (captain) and E. Osborne (team manager).
Parkin is holding the cup presented by the Sydney Tattersall's Club for competition between England and Australia.
The English team, who won two of the three Test matches, are the first holders of the trophy.

Left:
Farewell to Australia.
Leaving Sydney on the 'Aorangi' en route for New Zealand.

(Photograph courtesy Alf Ellaby).

Below:
Queen Street in Auckland.

An overwhelming rush by England, typical of their tactics throughout the game against South Auckland at Taupiri.

The First Test Match at Carlaw Park. Referee Bull (No.17) keeps a close watch at a ruck.

Harold leads out the team against Auckland.

The English actress Elsie Prince kicks off watched by Harold and Harold Young (far right).

Where Speed Counts - Rosser, the English three-quarter, bolting for the line, with L. Scott (extreme left), Hanlon and Amos in pursuit.

One of the fleet-footed Englishmen gets away.
Rosser puts in a brilliant run with his Auckland opponents in full cry. The Auckland Provincial team was defeated by 14 points to 9.

Bryn Evans secures the ball from a scrum with Auckland City's full back C. Dufty endeavouring to intercept.

Rosser and Fairclough bring down Wilson.

Bryn Evans brings down his opposite number Delgrosso with Fairclough (No.36) waiting to pounce.

England win the scrum to start a scoring move.

League Test in Dunedin marred by many infringements.
A snapshot as Burgess, an English forward, was being ordered off the field. The referee has taken Burgess by the arm and the line umpire is on the left.

Harold (far right) and seven of his team mates enjoying the sun in Honolulu.

(Photograph courtesy Alf Ellaby).

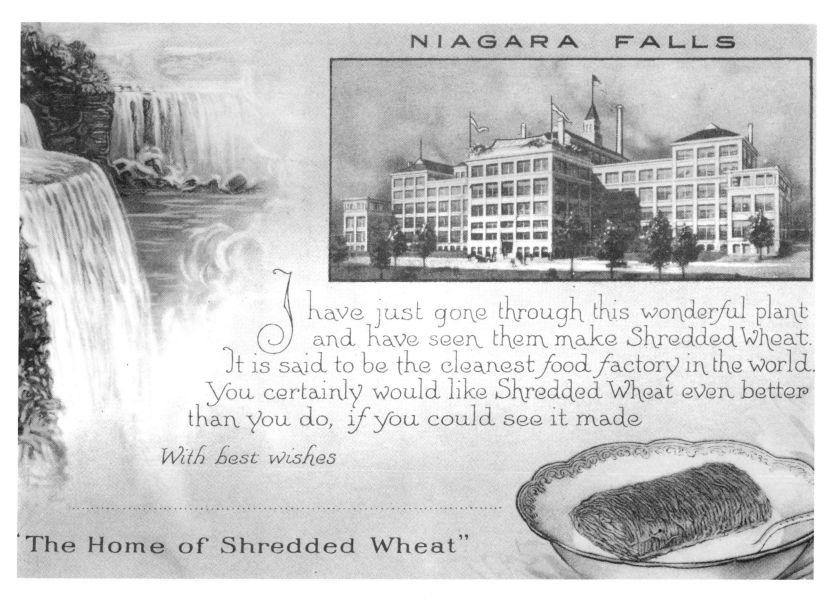

Niagara Falls Card.

Homeward bound on the 'Countess of Atholl'. Harold (right) enjoys his pipe.

1928 TOUR

MATCH RESULTS:

IN AUSTRALIA

South West Dist. (Cootamundra)	drew	14-14	8,000
New South Wales (Sydney)	lost	15-20	55,000
New South Wales (Sydney)	won	22-9	48,000
New South Wales (Sydney)	lost	7-22	38,000
Far Northern Coast (Lismore)	won	20-9	6,500
Queensland (Brisbane)	lost	7-21	25,000
Ipswich (Ipswich)	won	23-13	2,000
AUSTRALIA (Brisbane)	**won**	**15-12**	**39,200**
Central Queensland (Rockhampton)	won	27-11	10,000
Northern Queen sland (Townsville)	won	30-16	11,000
Wide Bay (Bundaberg)	won	61-13	4,000
Toowoomba (Toowoomba)	won	17-12	12,000
Newcastle (Newcastle)	won	19-17	7,000
AUSTRALIA (Sydney)	**won**	**8-0**	**44,548**
Western NSW (Parkes)	won	22-9	9,000
AUSTRALIA (Sydney)	**lost**	**14-21**	**37,000**

SUMMARY:
Played 16   Won 11   Lost 4   Drew 1
For
Tries 67   Goals 60   Points 321
Against
Tries 43   Goals 45   Points 219
Won Test series 2-1

IN NEW ZEALAND

South Auckland (Hamilton)	won	31-5	
NEW ZEALAND (Auckland)	**lost**	**13-17**	**28,000**
Auckland (Auckland)	won	14-9	15,000
Auckland City (Auckland)	won	26-15	25,000
Buller (Wesport)	won	72-3	
West Coast (Greymouth)	won	62-13	
NEW ZEALAND (Dunedin)	**won**	**13-5**	**12,000**
NEW ZEALAND (Christchurch)	**won**	**6-5**	**21,000**

An exhibition game against a New Zealand XIII was played at Invercargill, Britain losing 27-26, but this is not included in the tour records.

SUMMARY:
Played 8   Won 7   Lost 1
For
Tries 55   Goals 36   Points 237
Against
Tries 16   Goals 12   Points 72
Won Test series 2-1

TOUR TOTALS
Played 24   Won 18   Lost 5   Drew 1
For
Tries 122   Goals 96   Points 558
Against
Tries 59   Goals 57   Points 291

TOUR PARTY:

Managers: G. F. Hutchins (Oldham) and E. Osborne (Warrington)
Captain: J. Parkin (Wakefield T.)
Trainer: D. Murray

	App	Tries	Gls	Pts
T. Askin (Featherstone R.)	15	9	0	27
N. Bentham (Wigan Highfield)	14	1	0	3
F. Bowen (St. Helens Rec.)	16	2	0	6
H. Bowman (Hull)	14	2	0	6
J. Brough (Leeds)	15	6	0	18
W. Burgess (Barrow)	12	1	11	5
O. Dolan (St. Helens Rec.)	7	0	2	2
A. Ellaby (St. Helens)	14	20	0	64
B. Evans (Swinton)	12	1	0	3
J. Evans (Swinton)	3	1	0	3
L. Fairclough (St. Helens)	12	11	0	33
A. Fildes (St. Helens Rec.)	13	3	0	9
A. Frodsham (St. Helens)	17	15	25	45
W. Gowers (Rochdale H.)	9	0	0	50
T. E. Gwynne (Hull)	11	7	0	21
B. Halfpenny (St. Helens)	10	8	0	24
W. Horton (Wakefield T.)	15	5	0	15
J. Oliver (Batley)	9	4	0	12
J. Parkin (Wakefield T.)	4	2	0	6
W. Rees (Swinton)	19	4	0	12
M. Rosser (Leeds)	9	3	0	9
R. Sloman (Oldham)	12	4	0	12
J. Sullivan (Wigan)	15	3	52	113
J. Thompson (Leeds)	14	4	14	40
W. Williams (Salford)	12	0	1	2
H. Young (Bradford N.)	9	6	0	18

CONCLUSION

Harold was also chosen to tour Australia in 1932 but declined, officially for business and family reasons but more likely because he was disillusioned with the international scene. He continued playing for Hull F.C. until he retired in 1934. He made a total of 451 appearances and scored 75 tries, and played in eight Test Matches, v New Zealand (twice in 1924), v New Zealand (twice in 1926), v Australia (twice in 1928), v New Zealand (1928) and v Australia (1929). Scored one try.

For Yorkshire he played 13 times and scored 6 tries.

He captained Hull in season 1928-9 and made 24 appearances, scoring one try in derby matches against Hull Kingston Rovers in his career.

His son, Keith, signed for Hull from Hunslet in 1953 and made 149 appearances, scoring 90 tries for the club and made 4 appearances for Yorkshire, scoring one try.

In later life, Harold kept a pub, The Oddfellows Arms in Pocklington, farmed at Holme on Spalding Moor, ran a fish and chip shop and afterwards a turf accountancy business, both in Pocklington.

Harold collapsed in the West Stand at Boothferry Park, Hull on May 4th 1957. Hull F.C. were to meet Barrow in the League Play-off Semi-Final. He died immediately despite being rushed to the nearby Hull Royal Infirmary. Harold's other son, Keith, was in the Hull dressing room, being reserve for the match.

Harold was buried at All Saints Church in Pocklington on May 8th, the cortege leaving from 1 York View, Barmby Road, Pocklington. It was the end of a 36 year association with Hull Rugby Football Club.

Bill Westerdale (left) and Harold, opposing captains in the Hull Kingston Rovers v. Hull F.C. derby match, watched by referee R. Robinson, at Craven Park, April 18th, 1930. Hull F.C. won 11-3.

Harold and Eileen with sons George and Keith at the doorway of the Oddfellows Arms in Pocklington 1933.

Harold with sons George (wearing the cap), and Keith and holding daughter Iris in 1938.

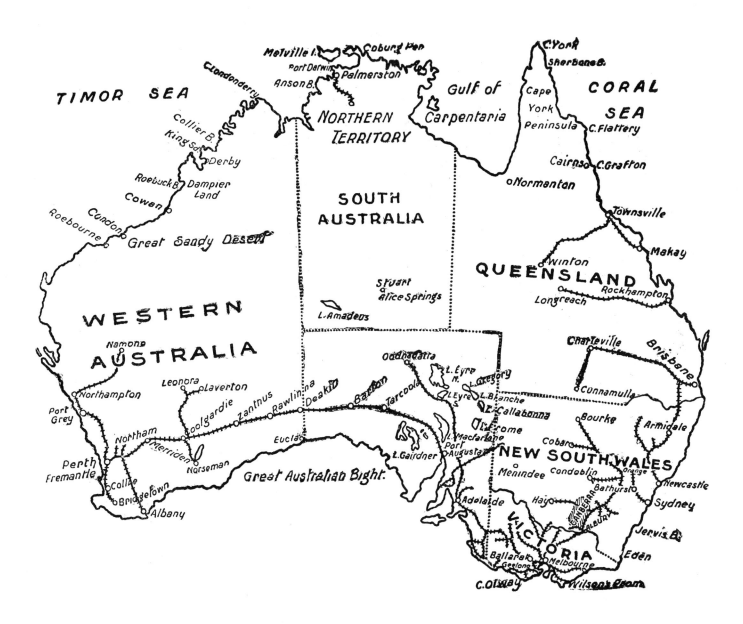